don't eat that lie

Exposing the Myths That Hold You Back and
Rewiring Your Mind for Success

dr alice ward-johnson

dedication

To the ones who have ever doubted their worth, questioned their potential, or believed the lies that tried to define them—this book is for you.

To my children, who have been my most profound motivation, you are proof that resilience and love can break every generational cycle.

To my husband, thank you for giving me the encouragement and space to pursue my dreams.

To my family and friends who have supported me through seasons of wilderness and breakthrough—thank you for seeing me even when I struggled to see myself.

To my younger self—who once believed she wasn't enough—I honor you for pushing through, unlearning the lies, and becoming the woman you were always meant to be.

And most of all, to God—who never left me, never forsook me, and whose truth I choose to consume.

This book is a call to freedom. Eat this truth.

With love and purpose,

Dr. Johnson

contents

the lies we consume

Let me ask you a question: How many lies have you eaten today?

Uhhh…what?!

I'm not talking about the food you've consumed—I'm talking about the thoughts, beliefs, and narratives you've allowed to settle in your mind.

Every day, our minds are flooded with thousands of thoughts—many of them on repeat. Studies suggest that many of these thoughts lean negative, reinforcing the same limiting beliefs and self-doubts we carried the day before. Without realizing it, we get caught in a cycle of mental patterns that hold us back. These thoughts often shape our reality. But here's the truth: You don't have to believe everything you think. It's time to challenge the lies.

But where do these lies come from? They are embedded in the messages we consume daily—social media, news, cultural expectations, and even the well-intended advice of those around us. We are constantly fed distorted standards, curated realities, and success stories that make us question our worth and abilities.

These lies are subtle, disguised as truths, and whispered into your subconscious by society, past experiences, and even your own inner critic. They tell you:

- *"You're not good enough."*
- *"It's too late for you."*
- *"You need approval to succeed."*
- *"You'll always struggle with money."*
- *"Everyone else has it figured out—why don't you?"*

But here's the truth: You are not defined by what others say about you—you are shaped by what you choose to believe.

This book is your wake-up call. It's your chance to stop consuming the mental junk food poisoning your potential and start feeding your mind with truths that empower, uplift, and transform.

why does this matter?

Your thoughts shape the blueprint of your life. Every belief you hold starts with a single thought. Every action you take will stem from it. Every outcome you experience is rooted in your thinking. If lies control your mind, they will control your life.

But the good news? You can rewrite the narrative. You can challenge those lies, replace them with empowering truths, and take control of your life in ways you never imagined.

Consider this: A single lie, left unchallenged, can cost you your dreams, your confidence, and your joy. Negative thinking isn't just a bad habit—it's a thief that steals your potential. But you don't have to let it. You can break the cycle, shift your mindset, and reclaim your future.

this book is your blueprint for transformation

I've been where you are. I've consumed the lies, let them take root, and watched as they tried to sabotage my dreams. But I've also discovered the antidote. Through my own experiences, lessons, and faith, I've learned how to challenge these common beliefs—these lies—and replace them with truths that help me live boldly and authentically.

And now, I'm here to share that journey with you.

Together, we'll explore how to:

- Identify the lies you've been fed.
- Understand how they've shaped your beliefs and actions.
- Break free from their grip by replacing them with truths that serve you.

This book isn't just about understanding lies—it's about actively rejecting them. It's about building the mental resilience to recognize deception before it takes root and training your mind to filter out the noise that keeps you stuck.

faith, identity, and transformation

Throughout these pages, we will explore profound truths about identity—who you truly are beyond the labels and limitations society tries to impose on you. We will dismantle the false beliefs that keep you stagnant and uncover the truth about your worth, potential, and purpose.

We will examine one of the most influential figures in the Bible: Peter. His story is a testament to what happens when you stop believing the world's lies and instead step into the truth of who God says you are. Peter had moments of doubt, fear, and failure, but his transformation shows us that our missteps don't define us—our faith does.

are you ready to change the narrative?

So, are you ready to take control of your mental nutrition? Are you ready to stop eating the lies and start feeding your mind with truths that transform?

If so, let's get started. Because the life you've been dreaming of is closer than you think. And it all begins with one simple decision:

Don't eat that lie.

the lies that hold us back

. . .

breaking free from the lies that limit you

Every day, we consume thoughts, beliefs, and narratives—some true, others harmful. Like processed junk food, lies are convenient and easy to absorb, offering temporary comfort but ultimately draining your energy, confidence, and ability to act. To reach your full potential, you must replace those lies with nourishing, life-giving truths.

Society, culture, and even well-meaning people have programmed us to believe certain myths about success, identity, and worth. These lies settle deep into our subconscious and often shape how we see ourselves without realizing it.

overcoming the need for approval

Before I started my tutoring center, I believed a common societal lie: "You need full support from your family and friends to be successful in business." I thought their encouragement was essential. However, when I opened my center, I noticed something surprising—some people closest to me, including those with children who could benefit from my services, didn't become my customers.

At first, this felt like rejection. I wondered, "If my family and friends don't believe in me, how can I succeed?" Doubt crept in, and I began second-guessing my ability to get customers.

But then I realized that my vision wasn't meant for them. My calling extended beyond my immediate circle. Just because my loved ones didn't immediately support me didn't mean my idea lacked value. I had to shift my focus to those who truly needed my services—those searching for academic support. This forced me to find "my customer."

Breaking free from this lie was liberating. It freed me from the need for external validation and allowed me to focus on my purpose with conviction, persistence, and faith.

common societal lies that hold us back

These self-limiting beliefs are everywhere, and they sound like this:

- "I have imposter syndrome. I'm not good enough."
- "If it hasn't been done before, It can't be done."
- "I can't pursue more than one career."
- "No one from my community has been successful, so I won't be either."
- "They won't let me succeed."
- "I'm not pretty enough, smart enough, talented enough."

how these lies take root

These lies don't emerge from nowhere; they are reinforced by cultural norms, media portrayals, and even well-meaning advice. Social media amplifies them. Over time, these narratives shape our subconscious beliefs, creating mental ruts that keep us stuck in fear and hesitation.

the cost of believing lies

Believing in these societal lies comes at a cost—one that many don't realize until they find themselves stuck in patterns of doubt, fear, and unfulfilled potential. These false narratives quietly drain your confidence, making you hesitate to take action or step outside your comfort zone. Each time you allow a limiting belief to take root, it creates a mental barrier that makes success feel further out of reach. You may question your abilities. Convinced that you do not deserve the opportunities before you.

Moreover, these lies rob you of joy, replacing contentment with a relentless comparison cycle. You may be scrolling through social media, measuring your life against carefully curated images of success and perfection. The result? Anxiety, self-doubt, and the constant feeling that you are falling short. These lies don't just affect how you feel; they stunt your growth by convincing you to play it safe and avoid risks. Over time, they condition you to believe that dreaming big is impractical and that success is reserved for a select few who were simply "born for it."

But here's the truth: these lies do not define you. The power to rewrite your story and change your perspective lies within you.

breaking free: your power to choose

You have the power to choose what you feed your mind. Just as you wouldn't fill your body with unhealthy food every day and expect to thrive, you must also be intentional about what you allow into your thoughts. What you consume mentally through conversations, media, and self-talk shapes your beliefs, influences your actions, and ultimately determines the life you create for yourself. If you continue to digest negativity, self-doubt, and false limitations, your reality will reflect those beliefs. But if you begin to nourish your mind with the belief that you are capable of more, you will start to see changes in your mindset and confidence. Over time, your life will shift in ways you never imagined possible.

It's time to control what you consume mentally and replace those lies with truth. You are more than the limitations society has placed on you. You are more than the doubts that whisper in your mind. Chapter 2 will explore how your mental diet affects your self-perception and actions. By understanding how to filter out negativity and intentionally fuel your mind with affirming beliefs, you will achieve clarity, confidence, and unstoppable potential.

exposing the lie of imposter syndrome

. . .

you deserve to be here. period.

Imposter syndrome is like artificial sweeteners—it tricks your mind into thinking you're inadequate when, in reality, you are thriving. It disguises itself as humility, whispering, "You don't belong here. You don't deserve this success. They'll find out you're a fraud." But let's call it what it is—a lie.

It thrives in moments of transition or growth when you step outside your comfort zone and into new challenges. You may feel undeserving of a promotion, unqualified for a leadership role, or doubtful about your ability to contribute to meaningful conversations. These thoughts create a mental barrier that makes you second-guess your skills and achievements, making it difficult to embrace the success you've rightfully earned.

The more you allow imposter syndrome to dictate your self-perception, the more you risk holding yourself back from opportunities that could change your life. It tricks you into believing you are an exception to success rather than a rightful participant. But the truth is, you belong in every room you step into, and your unique journey has equipped you to contribute in ways that no one else can.

facing the fraud feeling

I remember standing in front of a packed room, preparing to speak. Doubt flooded my mind. "What if they see right through me? What if I don't know as much about this as I think I do?" In times past, I was pretty confident in speaking about topics related to education and teaching because I had studied and gained degrees in this area. But now here I was, preparing to talk about a subject I had lived. I thought "I could talk about mindset, but do I need more certifications? Do I need a license? Maybe the audience would need someone more expert than me —a psychologist, a psychiatrist, or a professional counselor."

But then I remembered something—I had spent years preparing for this moment. I had lived the lessons I was about to share. My success was not an accident but the result of effort, persistence, and experience. I had overcome my mindset battles, which alone qualified me to stand on that stage. The lessons I learned weren't theoretical—they were real, tested through my challenges and growth. That realization grounded me, reminding me that my voice and journey mattered as much as any degree or title.

the lies imposter syndrome tells you

- **"Your success is just luck."** – But was it? Did you stumble into your achievements or work hard for them?
- **"You're not qualified."** – Qualification isn't about having all the answers; it's about the willingness to learn and grow.

- **"Everyone else has it all together—except you."** – Social media can make it seem that way, but nobody has it all figured out.
- **"You don't deserve to be here."** – If you weren't meant to be here, you wouldn't be.

the cost of believing the lie

Believing the lie of Imposter Syndrome doesn't just rob you of your joy—it robs the world of your gifts. When you shrink back and doubt your worth, you deny others the unique value only you can bring. Your hesitation becomes someone else's missed opportunity to benefit from your talents, ideas, and contributions.

Think about the ripple effect of your actions. When you step into your purpose and embrace your worth, you inspire others to do the same. Your courage can create a domino effect of empowerment and confidence. Conversely, when you dim your light, you reinforce the lie that others should dim theirs, too. The cost of Imposter Syndrome is not just personal—it's communal. The world needs what you have to offer, and it's time to stop holding back.

breaking down the lies of imposter syndrome

One of the most common lies that Imposter Syndrome tells you is that your success is just luck. It tries to convince you that everything you've achieved comes from chance rather than effort. But luck is random, and effort is deliberate. Consider your accomplishments: did you stumble upon that opportunity or position yourself for it? Did that promotion happen by accident or result from your skills, persistence, and dedication?

While timing might play a role in certain situations, your preparation and hard work ensure success.

Another insidious lie is that you're not qualified. This lie feeds off the notion that you must meet an ever-shifting standard to be considered worthy. However, qualification is a moving target, and genuine qualification often stems from a willingness to learn and grow. The actual frauds aren't the ones who doubt themselves but the ones who pretend to know it all. The real markers of competence are the courage to admit what you don't know and the determination to figure it out.

Imposter Syndrome also perpetuates the myth that everyone else has it together except you. It's easy to fall into this trap when comparing your behind-the-scenes struggles to someone else's highlight reel. Social media often amplifies this illusion, making it seem like everyone is effortlessly doing well in life while you're just trying to keep your head above water. But the truth is, nobody has it all together. Everyone is figuring it out as they go, and your vulnerability and self-awareness are strengths, not weaknesses.

Perhaps the most damaging lie is that you don't deserve to be where you are. Imposter Syndrome whispers that your presence in the room is a mistake, that you're out of place. But this is a falsehood that needs to be rejected outright. If you weren't meant to be here, you wouldn't be. Your journey, effort, and perseverance have led you to this moment. You belong because you've earned your place and your presence matters.

how to silence the imposter voice

The good news is that Imposter Syndrome can be silenced, and the first step is to own your wins. Stop downplaying your achievements or attributing them to external factors. When someone compliments your work, resist the urge to brush it off with, *"Oh, it was nothing."* Instead, simply say thank you and acknowledge the effort you put into earning that recognition. Your accomplishments are valid and deserve to be celebrated.

Another powerful strategy is to keep receipts of your success. Display your degrees and trophies. Celebrate your wins, both big and small. Keep records of the moments when you overcame challenges, exceeded expectations, or achieved something meaningful. When self-doubt creeps in, remind yourself of your capabilities and resilience. These practices build a strong case against the lies of Imposter Syndrome.

Reframing failure is also crucial in combating self-doubt. Failure isn't proof of inadequacy; it's proof of effort. The only people who don't fail are those who never try. Every failure is a lesson. Instead of viewing failure as a dead-end, see it as a valuable part of the process that leads to success.

In addition, using affirmations can help rewrite the narrative in your mind. Speak life into yourself with phrases like, *"I belong here. I am capable. My work has value. I am worthy."* Affirmations might feel awkward at first, but repetition makes them powerful. Over time, they can help you replace lies with truths and build a stronger foundation of self-belief.

Seeking perspective from trusted mentors, colleagues, or friends is another effective way to combat Imposter Syndrome. Sometimes, hearing someone else validate your worth can help you see yourself more clearly. They can provide a balanced perspective and remind you of the value you bring to the table.

I've learned the importance of surrounding myself with people who uplift and affirm me. Seek out those who celebrate your victories and cheer you on when you win. Find people who encourage you during setbacks and remind you that giving your best effort is what truly matters.

Finally, take action even when self-doubt lingers. The best way to silence Imposter Syndrome is to act in spite of it. Do it anyway. Do it afraid. Confidence isn't a prerequisite for action; it's a byproduct. Each step forward strengthens your confidence in your abilities. With every step, the lies that once held you back lose their power.

redefining success

Success isn't about being flawless; it's about showing up. It's about doing the work, learning, and making an impact. Every expert, leader, and innovator started somewhere, often filled with doubts and uncertainties. The difference between those who succeed and those who stay stuck in imposter syndrome is their willingness to take imperfect action.

When you embrace success as a journey of progress rather than a destination of perfection, you free yourself from the fear of making mistakes. Mistakes are not failures; they are stepping stones that refine your skills, deepen your understanding, and make you more resilient. Each time you take a step forward, no matter how small, you weaken the grip of imposter syndrome and reinforce your belief in yourself.

Redefining success means acknowledging that growth comes from experience, from trying, failing, adjusting, and trying again. It means celebrating the courage to start and the persistence to keep going. When you shift your mindset from "I have to be perfect" to "I have to keep learning and growing," you reclaim your power. The goal is not to have all the answers but to keep seeking them, improving, and showing up even when doubt lingers. That is the true measure of success.

Imposter Syndrome isn't a reflection of your ability—it's a reflection of your humanity. It is a universal experience felt by even the most accomplished individuals, from top executives to award-winning artists. The presence of doubt does not invalidate your achievements. Instead, it indicates that you are stretching beyond your comfort zone and taking on challenges that matter.

Feeling like an imposter doesn't mean you're failing; it means you're growing. Each new opportunity presents an internal battle between comfort and courage. But, choosing to push forward despite doubt sets successful individuals apart. Your journey is not about proving yourself to others. It's about embracing who you are and owning your unique perspective. Trust that your experiences, skills, and insights have value.

So, the next time Imposter Syndrome comes knocking, recognize it for what it is—a lie. Acknowledge the doubt but refuse to let it define you. Replace the whispers of insecurity with declarations of truth: *I am enough. I am capable. I am successful.* You belong here, and it's time you start believing it. Every room you step into, every opportunity you seize, and every challenge you conquer affirms your rightful place. Own your story, embrace your worth, and continue stepping boldly into the success that is already yours.

you are what you consume mentally

. . .

We've exposed the lies society feeds us and their power to limit our growth. But where do these lies take hold? Often, it's in the constant stream of mental inputs we consume daily. This chapter will examine how our mental diet shapes our beliefs and uncover strategies to nourish our minds with positivity and truth.

your mental diet shapes your reality

Just as you wouldn't eat spoiled or harmful food, you must filter what you allow into your mind. Your mental diet should be rich in uplifting, empowering inputs that strengthen your resilience and creativity while avoiding the toxic influences that drain you. The thoughts, ideas, and experiences you take in have a powerful impact. They shape your personality and influence both your beliefs and overall mental state. This concept reflects the quality of the mental "diet" you consume. Just like your physical health is influenced by the food you eat, your mental health is impacted by the information you expose yourself to.

The media you consume, the news you follow, the books you read, and the conversations you engage in all shape your perspective and worldview. Being selective about what you take in is an active choice that can dramatically shift your mindset. Filtering out negativity can positively influence your mental well-being, fostering a more optimistic outlook, just as nourishing food strengthens your body.

the influence of negativity

Negativity can creep into your life in subtle ways. Maybe it's a social media feed filled with complaints and drama. It could be a news cycle that amplifies fear and division. Or perhaps it's a circle of friends who focus on what's wrong instead of what's possible. Consuming these sources of negativity reinforces societal lies like, "My people will never be wealthy" or "Life is always harder for me." These harmful narratives take root and shape how you view yourself and your circumstances. Over time, these inputs become part of your mental diet, shaping your thoughts and emotions in ways you might not notice.

For instance, consuming a steady stream of alarming news can quickly lead to feelings of helplessness and anxiety. The first four minutes of the evening news can leave you feeling overwhelmed and hopeless. Consider how spending time around people who constantly criticize others can make you more critical, not just of others but of yourself. This is why being intentional about your mental inputs is so important. Consuming negativity reinforces lies like "The world is doomed" or "Things will never get better."

filtering your mental diet

To protect your mental health, you need to become an active participant in your mental consumption. This means:

- **Assessing Your Inputs:** Take stock of what you regularly consume. Are your social media feeds uplifting or draining? Does the music you listen to inspire or depress you?
- **Setting Boundaries:** Limit exposure to sources of negativity. For example, reduce time spent on social media platforms that trigger comparison. Disengage from conversations that leave you feeling drained.
- **Seek Positivity:** Surround yourself with uplifting content and people. Choose books, podcasts, and shows that motivate and encourage you. Build relationships with people who bring out the best in you.

the power of positive consumption

Positive inputs have the power to counteract negativity. When you choose content that inspires, educates, and uplifts, you strengthen empowering truths. For example, listening to a motivational podcast can remind you that your goals are within reach. Music that soothes or motivates can boost your mood and energy. Reading a personal growth book can provide strategies for overcoming challenges. Spending time with friends who celebrate your wins can build your confidence and self-worth.

Positive consumption can plant seeds of hope, creativity, and resilience. It reminds you that you have the power to shape your narrative and reject the lies that try to take root. When you make it a habit to nourish your mind with encouragement, education, and inspiration, your mindset shifts, making success more attainable and personal growth natural.

practical exercise: your mental inventory

Take a moment to reflect on your current mental diet. Identify one lie you've internalized through your mental "diet." Write down that lie and replace it with a truth that empowers you. For example, replace "I'm not good enough" with "I am capable and deserving of success." Next, reflect on these questions:

- What are you consuming daily (e.g., social media, news, books, conversations)?
- How does this content make you feel? Energized? Drained? Hopeful? Anxious?
- Identify one source of negativity you can reduce or eliminate and one source of positivity you can add.

closing reflection

The information you consume is powerful. It shapes how you see the world and how you see yourself. By choosing what you consume mentally, you reject the lie that you cannot change your perspective. Just as you wouldn't feed your body junk food every day, you shouldn't feed your mind a steady stream of negativity.

Choose wisely. Reject the lies. Nourish your mind with truth, hope, and positivity.

But what are these lies we need to reject? Society surrounds us with subtle and pervasive messages that often disguise themselves as truth. These common lies infiltrate our thoughts, shape our beliefs, and limit our potential. They tell us who we should be, what we should achieve, and how to measure our worth. To break free, we must first recognize these false narratives for what they are. In the next chapter, we'll look at some of the most prevalent lies society tells us and how they embed themselves into our thinking.

exposing the cultural lie

. . .

the truth hidden beneath the lies

Our cultural history is a feast of strength and resilience, but society often feeds us lies that distort this truth. Instead of swallowing these distortions, we must savor the richness of our roots and use them to fuel our journey forward. In the previous chapters, we tackled imposter syndrome and reclaimed our confidence in our abilities. But societal lies don't stop there— they often try to disconnect us from our roots and cultural heritage. This chapter will show how embracing our history, rather than denying it, can become a foundation for strength and resilience.

Too often, society perpetuates the false idea that to succeed, we must distance ourselves from our cultural history. This lie is especially harmful to African Americans, as it suggests that the rich and complex history of our ancestors is a burden rather than a source of power. The truth is this: our cultural history— our roots—does not hold us back. It propels us forward.

unpacking the lie

This lie convinces us that the challenges and traumas of our past dictate our future. For African Americans, it often manifests in three harmful ways:

- The dismissal or downplaying of African-American contributions to history and culture creates the false impression that our heritage lacks value or significance.
- The ongoing effects of systemic racism can make success seem unattainable, reinforcing the belief that the odds are too heavily stacked against us.
- These external messages often lead to self-doubt, making us feel that we must constantly prove our worth and justify our success.

This lie disconnects us from the strength, creativity, and resilience embedded in our heritage. It convinces us to see our history as a burden rather than a source of empowerment.

the truth: your cultural history is a foundation, not a limitation

Our cultural history is a foundation—a source of strength and resilience that equips us for greatness. As descendants of the strongest Africans who survived the transatlantic slave trade, African Americans are living proof of unyielding hope and perseverance.

Strength in Struggle

Our history is a testament to overcoming insurmountable odds. From the horrors of slavery to the victories of the civil rights movement, African Americans have continually demonstrated extraordinary resilience. This legacy is our inheritance, a reminder that we can face and conquer any challenge.

I remember the first time I truly connected with the strength of my cultural history. My grandfather was part of the Great Migration, a time in the early 20th century when millions of African Americans left the South searching for better opportunities in the North and West. In the early 1950s, he moved his family from Mississippi to Wisconsin to pursue a better life, determined to carve out a promising future.

When he arrived in Wisconsin, he opened his own business and worked tirelessly to build a loyal customer base. Despite the racial barriers and economic hardships of the time, he successfully ran and grew that business for over 30 years. As an African American man, I'm sure he faced unimaginable adversity in the beginning. Yet, through determination, hard work, and resilience, he thrived. His story was more than just history—it was a blueprint for perseverance. It showed me that resilience was in my DNA, that I was never alone in my struggles, and that my ancestors had already paved the way for me to succeed.

Inspiration in Excellence

African Americans have made groundbreaking contributions in every field: medicine, law, science, literature, music, sports, and politics. These achievements prove the unlimited potential within our community, from Katherine Johnson's calculations that propelled space exploration to Maya Angelou's words that inspired millions. Their success demonstrates that greatness is not confined by circumstance but unleashed through determination.

Community in Shared Experience

The collective experiences of the African American community, both painful and celebratory, create a deep well of wisdom and motivation. Traditions, stories, and shared victories unite us, offering lessons that fuel our drive to achieve even more. Embracing this shared history strengthens our sense of belonging and reminds us that we are part of something greater than ourselves.

the reframe: your history equips you for success

Instead of seeing cultural history as a limitation, view it as a blueprint for success. Your history does not determine your destiny—it prepares you for it. The same strength, creativity, and ingenuity that allowed our ancestors to endure and thrive flow through you. You are not bound by your history; you are empowered by it.

turning truth into momentum

Rather than treating history as something to be remembered from a distance, we should actively apply its lessons. Here's how you can turn cultural truth into personal momentum:

1. **Research Your Roots**
   - Learn about how your ancestors have shaped history. Read their stories, study their journeys, and understand the principles that guided them. Their resilience and achievements can inspire and inform your path forward.
2. **Celebrate Your Heritage**
   - Embrace your cultural identity as a source of pride. Incorporate traditions, art, and values from your heritage into your life. Whether through music, food,

or storytelling, honoring your history strengthens your connection to the power of your roots.

3. **Share the Story**
    - Pass down the lessons of your heritage, especially to younger generations. Help them see their cultural history as a source of strength and possibility. By sharing these stories, you ensure that the legacy of resilience and excellence continues to inspire.

4. **Apply the Lessons of the Past**
    - Explore the principles that guided past generations: perseverance, adaptability, and collective empowerment. These lessons are timeless and can help us overcome modern challenges.

personal reflection

Take a moment to reflect on how your cultural history has shaped you. What lessons have you drawn from the struggles and triumphs of those before you? What strengths have you inherited from their experiences? How can you use this foundation to pursue your dreams?

Think about the ways your heritage equips you to succeed. Ask yourself: How can I honor my ancestors' resilience by living a life of purpose and achievement?

don't eat that lie

The lie that your cultural history limits your destiny is nothing more than a tool to hold you back. The truth is that your heritage fuels your potential and propels you toward greatness. You are proof of your ancestors' resilience, creativity, and brilliance.

final thoughts

As a minority, I understand the weight of this lie and how it can create moments of doubt. But I also know the power of embracing cultural history as a source of strength. It is not always easy to rewrite the false narratives that society has written, but it is essential.

When you feel the weight of that lie creeping in, remind yourself: *I am more than my struggles. I am more than the challenges I face. I am the result of generations of strength, resilience, and hope.*

Your cultural history does not determine your destiny; it equips you for it. Embrace the truth, honor your heritage, and let the resilience of your ancestors propel you toward the greatness that awaits you. Don't eat that lie.

the weight of words

. . .

We uncovered the cultural lie that attempts to disconnect us from our history and identity. Now, we turn to the influence of our past, specifically the words spoken over us by those closest to us. This chapter will empower you to break free from limiting labels and step into the truth of your inherent worth.

Growing up, we often view our parents as the ultimate authority figures. They're our first teachers, our earliest examples of love and care, and the voices we usually hear in our formative years. Because of this, the words they speak carry tremendous weight. Sometimes, these words uplift and encourage. But other times, they plant seeds of doubt and insecurity that can grow into lifelong struggles. The lie that the negative statements of your parents define your worth is one of the most pervasive and harmful lies you can believe.

the impact of parental labels

A friend once told me a story about their father, who often said, "You're stupid." At the time, my friend didn't fully understand how much those words would affect them. These statements were harsh corrections of misbehavior or expressions of parental frustration. But as he grew older, those words began to take root, shaping how he saw himself and his potential.

In school, he excelled in some areas but struggled in others. Each time he faced challenges, those words from his father echoed in his mind, reinforcing the idea that he wasn't smart enough to succeed. Even as an adult, he carried this insecurity into his career and relationships, often second-guessing decisions and avoiding challenges. He frequently dismisses compliments about his intelligence. It wasn't until much later in life that he realized the words of his father were not the truth but rather reflections of his father's frustrations or his own unresolved issues.

The same is true for many people. A girl might grow up believing she's not pretty because her mother repeatedly said, "You'll never be as pretty as your sister," or "You're too dark to wear that." A boy might feel incapable of achieving greatness because his parents constantly compared him to others, saying, "Why can't you be more like them?" These simple statements, often said without much thought, can become lies that shape how we see ourselves and what we believe we can achieve.

breaking the lie

The first step in breaking free from the lie that your parents' statements define you is recognizing that their words are not absolute truths. They are opinions, shaped by their own experiences, frustrations, and sometimes, their own unhealed wounds. Understanding this doesn't mean dismissing your parents entirely or excusing hurtful behavior. It means separating their words from your identity.

When you challenge these lies, you'll see that your worth isn't tied to anyone else's opinion of you—not even your parents. You are not stupid, ugly, incapable, or unworthy simply because someone said so. Your value is inherent, given by God, and unchanging regardless of others' words.

practical strategies for overcoming the impact of negative statements

1. Identify the Lies You've Believed

Start by writing down the negative statements you remember from your parents. For each statement, ask yourself:

- Is this true?
- What evidence do I have to support or refute this?
- How has believing this statement affected my life?

By identifying the specific lies you've internalized, you can begin to separate them from the truth about who you are.

2. Replace the Lies with Truth

For every lie, write a truth to counter it. For example:

- Lie: "You're not smart enough."
- Truth: "I am intelligent and capable. My abilities are not defined by someone else's opinion."

Repeat these truths to yourself daily. Affirmations can help rewire your thinking and replace negative self-beliefs with positive ones.

3. Seek Validation from Within

Learn to validate yourself instead of seeking validation from others. Celebrate your accomplishments, no matter how small, and remind yourself of your strengths. You don't need external approval to know your worth.

4. Surround Yourself with Positive Influences

Spend time with people who uplift and encourage you. Their positive reinforcement can help drown out the negative voices from your past. Choose mentors, friends, or books and podcasts that inspire and motivate you.

5. Heal Through Forgiveness

Forgiveness doesn't mean excusing hurtful behavior or pretending it didn't happen. It means letting go of the anger and resentment that keep you tied to those painful words. Forgive your parents for their shortcomings and release the power their words have held over you.

6. Seek Professional Support

Therapy or counseling can be incredibly helpful in unpacking the impact of negative parental statements. A professional can guide you through the healing process and help you build a healthier self-image.

embracing your true identity

As my friend worked through his own journey, he realized that his father's words did not define his intelligence or worth. He began challenging those lies and embracing the truth about who he is. He started pursuing opportunities that once felt out of reach. He took on challenges that required confidence in his abilities. And he learned to celebrate his successes without second-guessing them.

For the girl who was told she wasn't pretty, the journey might involve looking in the mirror and affirming her beauty daily. She might focus on her unique features, celebrate her inner qualities, and reject societal standards that don't define her. For the boy who was told he wasn't capable, it might mean setting goals, achieving them, and recognizing that his worth isn't tied to comparisons.

final thoughts

Your parents' words have power, but they do not have the final say over your life. You are not the sum of their criticisms or offhand remarks. You are a unique, valuable, and capable individual with unlimited potential. By identifying and challenging the lies you've believed, replacing them with truth, and seeking healing, you can break free from the negative impact of parental statements and live a life that reflects your true worth.

Remember, others do not define your identity. It is determined by the truth of who you are—a truth that is unshakable, undeniable, and uniquely yours. The labels others place on you do not have to be the ones you carry forward. You have the power to rewrite your story and to define yourself by your strengths.

rejecting the lie: "you're selfish"

. . .

Prioritizing yourself isn't selfish; it's choosing a balanced mental diet. Just as your body needs nourishment to function, your mind and soul need care to show up fully for others. Feeding yourself with self-care first isn't an indulgence—it's a necessity.

---

the truth about prioritizing yourself

We addressed the impact of labels placed on us by our parents and how their words do not define us forever. Now, we turn to another deeply ingrained lie: the belief that prioritizing yourself makes you selfish. This chapter will reveal why self-care is necessary and the key to showing up for others in meaningful ways.

Many of us have been fed the lie that prioritizing yourself makes you selfish. This lie often convinces people to put everyone else's needs ahead of their own, leaving them exhausted, unfulfilled, and often resentful. While it's noble to want to help others, the truth is that you cannot pour from an empty cup. You must invest in yourself daily to show up for others meaningfully.

a reflection on selfishness

There was a time in my life when I found myself at odds with a family member over this very idea. They accused me of always thinking about myself and making everything about me. Initially, I was deeply hurt by their words. After all, I had spent so much of my life pouring into others. I'd been the one who showed up, the one who sacrificed, the one who tried to solve everyone's problems. Whether it was motivating someone to pursue their goals, teaching them something new, or simply being a listening ear, I had given so much of myself to the people around me.

Yet, as I considered what was said, I realized something profound. While the accusation wasn't entirely true, a kernel of truth was buried in their words. In some ways, I had made my life about others to the point of losing myself. I became an enabler, helping people who weren't ready to help themselves and often ignoring my needs. I was burning out, and the cycle wasn't sustainable.

That season of loneliness forced me to reexamine my life and priorities. I began to ask myself tough questions: Why was I so focused on fixing others? What would happen if I poured that same energy into fixing myself? The answers were uncomfortable initially, but they led to a powerful revelation: I had to make my life about me—not self-centered or egotistical, but in a way that allowed me to become the best version of myself—for myself and the people I cared about.

I started to do just that. I began focusing on my own healing, growth, and happiness. I stopped trying to fix other people's lives or solve their challenges. Instead, I shifted to helping where my help was truly wanted and praying for the rest. It was liberating. I no longer felt the pressure to be everything for everyone. I could show up for others in healthier, more intentional ways because I had taken the time to show up for myself first.

I also had to learn to leave people where they were. Maybe they didn't want help. If they didn't want my help or want to change, I had to let them be themselves. Another hard pill was realizing that some people wanted help—but not from me. I had to learn how to be okay with that. I also learned that the people I was put on this earth to help may not be in my circle and that those who needed me would find me.

the power of prioritizing yourself

When you prioritize yourself, you're not being selfish but responsible. Taking care of yourself physically, emotionally, mentally, and spiritually enables you to:

- Set healthy boundaries by recognizing your limits and communicating them effectively to others
- Show up fully because your needs are met, allowing you to engage with others without feeling depleted
- Model self-care and create a ripple effect that fosters healthier relationships and communities
- Maintain peace and balance even amid chaos.

practical strategies for putting yourself first

If you're ready to embrace this truth, here are some practical strategies to help you prioritize yourself without guilt:

1. Reframe Your Mindset

Recognize that focusing on yourself isn't about neglecting others but equipping yourself to serve them better. Think of it like the safety instructions on an airplane: you must put on your oxygen mask before helping others. When you're at your best, you can give your best.

2. Set Clear Boundaries

Learn to say no when needed. Saying no doesn't make you unkind; it makes you honest. Not every request for your time or energy deserves a yes. Decide what aligns with your priorities and values, and let that guide your decisions.

3. Schedule "Me Time" Every Day

Self-care is not just for certain days. Block out time on your calendar for yourself. This isn't about an occasional self-care day; this is about carving out space every single day. Whether in the morning or evening, dedicate time to rest, read, pursue a hobby, exercise, meditate, or do anything that rejuvenates you.

4. Focus on Quality Over Quantity

When you do help others, focus on quality interactions. Be fully present and engaged. It's better to give someone your undivided attention for a short time than to be distracted and drained over a long period.

5. Reflect and Reassess

Periodically check in with yourself. Are you prioritizing your needs? Are you overextending yourself to help others? Adjust as needed to maintain a healthy balance.

6. Practice Gratitude and Prayer

Start and end your day with gratitude. Thank God for the opportunity to grow, heal, and show up as your best self. Pray for guidance in discerning how to help others without sacrificing your well-being.

the shift in helping others

Now, when I help others, it's different. I don't jump in to fix their problems or carry their burdens. Instead, I:

- Listen without judgment and offer my presence and compassion without feeling the need to provide solutions
- Ask how I can help rather than assuming I know what's best for them
- Respect their journey, and understand that everyone's path is unique and may look different from what I would choose
- Trust God with the rest, lifting them in prayer when I've done all I can

embracing the "selfish" label

When you prioritize yourself, some people might still label you selfish. That's okay. Let them. What matters is that you're living a life that aligns with your values and allows you to thrive. By putting yourself first, you're transforming your own life and showing others what's possible when you lead with authenticity and self-love.

Remember, life is about you. It's about your growth, your purpose, and your journey. When you honor that truth, you become a source of light and strength for others—not because you're running on empty, but because you're overflowing with the goodness you've cultivated within yourself.

final thoughts

The lie that prioritizing yourself is selfish is one of the most pervasive and damaging beliefs we can hold. It keeps us stuck in cycles of overgiving, burnout, and frustration. But the truth is liberating: when you focus on yourself, you empower yourself to show up as your best version. And that version of you—healthy, whole, and grounded—is precisely what the world needs.

So take the time to pour into yourself. Fix the things in your life that need fixing. Love yourself enough to make your life about you. Because when you do, you'll find that you're not only helping yourself—you're helping everyone around you in ways you never imagined.

the myth of perfection

. . .

Pursuing perfection is like chasing the newest fad diet—it's unsustainable and harmful. God doesn't demand perfection; He asks for authenticity. Feed your mind with grace, not guilt, and let go of the lie that you must earn His love.

---

letting go of the need to be perfect

With the myth of selfishness debunked, we now shift our focus to another equally paralyzing belief: the pursuit of perfection. Releasing the pressure to be flawless deepens one's relationship with God and oneself. Embracing imperfection becomes a vital part of one's growth and journey.

I've been attending church since I was a child, and Sunday Services are a regular part of my life. But as much as I loved attending church, I've seen my share of mess. There were times when people said things or did things that hurt me deeply—so deeply that I left particular churches as a result.

For a long time, I couldn't separate those experiences from my relationship with God. I started to question whether this was what faith was supposed to feel like. At times, I felt frustrated, confused, and even angry. I wondered if my struggle to fit into a church community meant I was somehow failing in my faith.

But as I grew older, I realized something that completely changed my perspective: It wasn't God who hurt me; it was people. People are human—they make mistakes, say the wrong things, and sometimes lose sight of God's heart. That realization helped me separate the spiritual from the natural. It allowed me to see that my faith wasn't about them; it was about me and God.

Some of my greatest moments with God have been outside of church. On my job, in my kitchen, the moments in the car by myself are unforgettable. In the stillness of my mornings, when I'm in bed before anyone wakes up, I've felt His presence so clearly, so profoundly. Those moments taught me that church is not the only place God shows up. He's with me everywhere, in every situation, ready to meet me right where I am.

Maybe God allowed me to experience hurt in the church so I could see that my relationship with Him is personal. It's mine. When I finally understood that, the actions of others couldn't keep me away from Him any longer.

the pressure to be perfect

Many of us grow up believing that to be worthy of God's love, we must live a perfect life—free of mistakes, doubts, or shortcomings. We believe that if we don't measure up, we're somehow failing Him. But this couldn't be further from the truth.

God never called us to be perfect; He called us to be faithful. He called us to trust Him, to walk with Him, and to allow Him to shape us through life's experiences. When we embrace this truth, we begin to see our flaws not as failures but as opportunities for growth.

One morning, during my time with God, I felt the weight of imperfection lift. It wasn't about being flawless—it was about being present. I realized that God's love wasn't something I had to earn. It was already there, waiting for me to accept it. That moment changed everything. I stopped striving for perfection and started seeking a deeper connection with Him.

practical steps to replace the lie with the truth

1. Stop Striving for Perfection
You don't have to earn God's love; He's already given it freely. Let go of the pressure to have it all together. God works best when imperfect people are willing to say, "Here I am, Lord."

2. Don't Let People Push You Away
People might criticize, gossip, or disappoint you, but don't let their actions turn you away from God's love. Fix your eyes on Him, not them. They don't hold your destiny—He does.

3. Redefine What Church Means
Church isn't about checking a box or meeting someone else's standard. It's a place to reconnect, refocus, and be filled. Don't see it as a requirement; see it as an opportunity to grow closer to God.

4. Focus on the Spirit, Not the People
People can hurt you, but God never will. Separate the spiritual from the natural and trust that God's Spirit is always for you, even when people fall short.

5. Spend Time with God Daily
Build your relationship with God outside of church. Pray, reflect on His goodness, and invite Him into your daily life. The more time you spend with Him, the stronger your relationship will become.

6. Forgive and Let Go
Don't let bitterness from past experiences weigh you down. Forgive those who hurt you—not because they deserve it, but because you refuse to let them keep you from God's best for your life.

7. Keep Moving Forward
When people try to discourage you or when life gets tough, don't stop. Keep chasing after God, knowing He has great things in store for you. He can take your pain and turn it into purpose.

embracing imperfection as part of your journey

We often think of biblical figures as flawless heroes, but the reality is that they were imperfect people who trusted God despite their struggles. Moses doubted himself, David made serious mistakes, and Peter denied Jesus three times, yet God still used them in powerful ways.

The same is true for us. God is not waiting for us to become perfect before He moves in our lives. He meets us where we are, flaws and all, and walks with us on our journey. The sooner we embrace this, the more we'll experience His peace, grace, and love.

I remember when I hesitated to step into opportunities because I felt unqualified. I wondered if I was good enough, knowledgeable enough, or prepared enough. But each time, God reminded me that He wasn't looking for perfection—He was looking for my willingness. As I took those steps in faith, He equipped me.

closing reflection

You don't have to be perfect to have a relationship with God. He's not looking for perfection; He's looking for your heart. Don't let the actions of others keep you from experiencing His love. Church isn't the requirement—it's the byproduct. It's where you can refocus, reconnect, and receive what your spirit needs. But most of all, remember that God is with you right now, just as you are.

When you embrace the truth that you are already enough in His eyes, you free yourself from the exhausting pursuit of perfection. You begin to live confidently, knowing His grace is sufficient for you. Let go of the lie. Walk boldly in the truth. And trust that God's love for you is unwavering, no matter what.

the bridge between lies

. . .

External lies are like enticing advertisements for junk food, while internal lies are the cravings we develop for them. Recognizing this cycle allows us to break free and choose a mental diet filled with truth and empowerment.

---

the intersection of external and internal lies

Now that we've dismantled the myth that perfection is necessary for worthiness, we must explore another deceptive force—the intersection of societal lies and our internal deceptions. This chapter acts as a bridge, shifting our focus from external influences to the lies we tell ourselves, beginning with one of the most dangerous: "I'll do it later."

Lies surround us, shaping the way we see the world and ourselves. Society tells us we're not enough, that our worth is tied to perfection or external approval, and that our circumstances dictate our identity. These societal lies infiltrate our thoughts, influencing how we navigate life. But there's a deeper layer—a second wave of deception that comes from within. These are the lies we tell ourselves, often subconsciously, to avoid discomfort, fear, or uncertainty. They feel safer than facing the truth of who we are and what we can achieve.

the connection between external lies and internal deceptions

The lies society tells us are the foundation for the ones we create. When the world teaches you that you're not smart, pretty, or worthy enough, your inner dialogue begins to echo these sentiments. You might say to yourself:

- *"I'll wait until I'm more prepared before starting my dream project."*
- *"I'll focus on myself later once things calm down."*
- *"It's not the right time to try something new; I must wait for better circumstances."*

These thoughts stem from external messages we absorb but become self-imposed barriers over time. You begin to weave them into the fabric of your identity, believing that hesitation and delay are justified. This is where societal and internal lies meet, forming a loop that keeps you stuck.

Take, for instance, the lie that success requires perfection. Society glorifies flawless achievements, and you internalize the belief that any misstep disqualifies you. So, instead of trying, you tell yourself you'll start when you're *"ready"*—a readiness that never seems to arrive.

Or consider the belief that other people's validation determines your worth. If society teaches you that approval is everything, you might procrastinate on your goals out of fear of failure or judgment. The lie *"I'll do it later"* becomes a shield, protecting you from potential rejection.

In both cases, the root lies may have originated externally, but the damage continues because of the lies you tell yourself.

the illusion of "later"

Let's examine the lie of *"I'll do it later"* more closely. At its core, it's a form of self-deception that offers comfort in the short term while robbing you of long-term growth. It gives you the illusion of control, making you believe that delaying action is being careful or strategic. But in reality, *"later"* is often a mask for fear, doubt, or a lack of commitment.

Why do we cling to this lie? The reasons vary:

- **Fear of Failure:** If you never start, you never have to face the possibility of failing. The lie protects you from vulnerability but also prevents you from growing.
- **Perfectionism:** You convince yourself that conditions must be ideal before taking action. Waiting becomes a way to avoid imperfection.
- **Overwhelm:** When goals feel too big, breaking them down seems daunting. Postponement becomes a coping mechanism for avoiding discomfort.
- **False Optimism:** We often believe we'll have more time, energy, or resources in the future. This misplaced confidence keeps us stuck in a cycle of delay.

The cost of this lie is immense. Every time you say, *"I'll do it later,"* you sacrifice an opportunity to move closer to your dreams. You trade action for stagnation, progress for regret. The longer you wait, the more insurmountable the task appears until *"later"* becomes *"never."*

from societal lies to self-awareness

Recognizing the transition from external lies to internal ones requires self-awareness. Ask yourself:

- *Which societal lies have I internalized? (For example, "I'm not good enough" or "It's too late for me.")*
- *How have these beliefs shaped my self-talk?*
- *What excuses do I make to justify inaction?*

Understanding these connections allows you to see the bigger picture. External lies may have set the stage, but the internal lies keep you stuck in the wings, never stepping into the spotlight.

the power of now

The antidote to *"I'll do it later"* is deceptively simple: action. Not perfect action, not monumental action—just one small step in the right direction. The truth is, you don't need more time, resources, or preparation. You need the courage to start, even if it feels messy or uncertain.

Consider this: What could you accomplish if you stopped waiting for *"later"*? What dreams could you bring to life if you refused to let fear or doubt dictate your timeline? The power lies in the present moment—the only moment you truly have.

a reflection exercise

Before moving into the next chapter, take a moment to reflect on the following questions:

- *What is one thing you've been putting off because you've told yourself, "I'll do it later"?*
- *What external lies may have influenced this delay?* (e.g., societal pressure, cultural narratives)
- *What small action could you take today to begin dismantling this lie?*

Write your answers down and commit to revisiting them. Let this reflection bridge you from hesitation to action, from societal lies to self-truth.

closing thoughts

The lies society tells us create a web of doubt, fear, and insecurity, but the lies we tell ourselves are the threads that keep us entangled. To break free, we must address both. The journey begins with recognizing that the greatest lie isn't the one we hear from the world—it's the one we repeat to ourselves: *"I'll do it later."*

As you turn the page, we'll confront this lie head-on. We'll explore why it's so dangerous, how it holds us back, and what we can do to replace it with empowering truths. Remember, the time to act is now. Let's dismantle this lie and reclaim the power of the present.

lies we tell ourselves about time

. . .

The lie 'I'll do it later' is like skipping meals—it seems harmless but leaves you depleted. Taking action now is like eating when you're hungry: it fuels your growth and keeps you moving forward.

---

breaking free from the illusion of "later"

We've explored the connection between external and internal lies. Now it's time to dive deeper into one of our most insidious lies: "I'll do it later." This delay comes at a hidden cost, often keeping us from turning dreams into reality. By confronting procrastination head-on, we can shift from intention to action and create real change.

"I'll do it later." It's a simple phrase we've all uttered at some point. It feels harmless, even comforting, like a promise to ourselves that we'll eventually get to the things that matter. But hidden beneath those four words is one of the most dangerous lies we can believe. *"Later"* often turns into days, weeks, or even years, and the opportunity to act slips through our fingers. The truth is tomorrow is not promised. The only moment we truly have is the one we're in right now.

the cost of "later"

I remember speaking with a colleague who always talked about writing a book. She had brilliant ideas, stories that could inspire, and a unique perspective the world needed to hear. But every time I encouraged her to start, she'd say, "I'll do it later when I'm less busy." Months turned into years, and life didn't slow down for her. The demands of work, family, and everyday obligations piled up. When she finally felt ready to write, she faced unexpected health challenges that drained her energy and focus. The book she'd dreamed of writing never came to life, all because she believed the lie that there would always be time later.

We all have our version of that story. It might not be a book; it could be a business idea, a phone call to a loved one, or even a decision to prioritize our health. Whatever it is, the lie of *"later"* robs us of the chance to live fully in the present and build our desired future.

"The best time to plant a tree was 20 years ago. The second-best time is now."

This African proverb beautifully captures the urgency of taking action. It reminds us that while we can't change the past, we can decide to act today. The seeds of our actions today determine the fruit we'll harvest tomorrow. Waiting delays the growth and blessings meant for us.

the cost of procrastination

Procrastination isn't just a harmless delay; it's a thief that steals our time, dreams, and opportunities. Here are some of the hidden costs of believing the lie:

- **Missed Opportunities** – Opportunities don't always come around twice. Delaying action can mean losing chances that may never return.
- **Increased Stress** – Pushing things off often leads to a pile-up of responsibilities, creating unnecessary stress and anxiety.
- **Regret** – Looking back on what could have been is one of life's most significant sources of regret.
- **Stunted Growth** – Every time we delay action, we delay growth. Whether it's personal development, career advancement, or relationships, procrastination keeps us stuck.

practical strategies to overcome the "later" lie

1. Start Small
Big goals can feel overwhelming, which makes procrastination tempting. Break your goal into smaller, manageable steps and focus on starting rather than finishing. Progress is better than perfection.

2. Set Deadlines
Give yourself a timeline for each task, even if it's self-imposed. Deadlines create a sense of urgency and accountability, helping you stay on track.

3. Eliminate Distractions

Identify the things that pull your attention away from what matters. Whether it's social media, TV, or endless scrolling, minimize distractions to create space for focused action.

4. Use the Two-Minute Rule
If something takes less than two minutes to do, do it immediately. This habit can help you tackle small tasks quickly and build momentum for larger ones.

5. Visualize the Outcome
Imagine the sense of accomplishment and joy you'll feel when you complete what you've been putting off. Use that positive energy as motivation to start.

6. Create a Daily Routine
Incorporate your goals into your daily routine. Consistent action, even if small, leads to significant results over time.

7. Seek Accountability
Share your goals with someone you trust and ask them to hold you accountable. Having a supportive partner can keep you motivated and focused.

the truth behind the "later" lie

Later, when I'm ready—
The sweetest lie we tell,
A whispered self-deception
We've come to know so well.
"Later, I'll be stronger,"
We promise in the night.
"Later, I'll be braver,
The timing will be right."

"Later, I'll have wisdom
That now I seem to lack.
Later, all my doubts will fade"—
False prayers we whisper back.
We tell ourselves that someday
The stars will align just so,
That future-perfect versions
Of us will surely know.
"Later, I'll deserve it,"
We bargain with our dreams.
"Later, I'll be worthy"—
Not seeing what this means.
For every "later" spoken
Is "never" in disguise,
A comfortable fiction,
The gentlest of lies.
We paint our future selves
As giants we can't be,
While present moments vanish
Into history.
The truth hides in the mirror:
We're ready as we'll be.
The self we're always waiting for
Is who we are to see.
For "later" is a lockbox
Where dreams go to expire,
While "now" remains the only key
To all that we desire.
So let us shed this comfort,
This sweetened poison sip,
And grasp the raw and ready truth:
Now's our strongest grip.

embracing the truth

The truth is action is the antidote to procrastination. When we take even the smallest step toward our goals, we reclaim our power from the lie of *"later."* Every step forward builds momentum, making the next step easier. By acting now, we're not just addressing tasks; we're shaping our futures and honoring the gifts we've been given.

final thoughts

The lie of *"I'll do it later"* is a subtle but powerful trap that keeps us from living fully. But we can break free from its grip by recognizing the truth and taking deliberate action. As the African proverb reminds us, *the second-best time to plant a tree is now.* So plant your seeds, take steps, and create the life you want today because the present moment is all we truly have.

action over thought

. . .

Action is the main course in your mental nutrition plan. Thinking alone is like staring at a menu without ordering—it won't fill you up. Acting on your goals nourishes your growth and satisfies your potential.

turning thought into action

We explored how procrastination robs us of our potential. Now, we shift from hesitation to empowerment. Taking action—not just gaining awareness—is the key to silencing lies and building momentum toward lasting change.

Awareness is the foundation of transformation. It begins with observing your thoughts and understanding their patterns. Then, you work to catch negative thoughts before they take root. This process allows you to interrupt the lies that threaten to derail your progress and replace them with empowering truths.

the power of mindfulness and reframing

Negative thought patterns often operate on autopilot, shaping how we see ourselves and the world without realizing it. These patterns include self-doubt, fear of failure, and catastrophic thinking. I've lived this reality. For years, I let a constant, nagging voice in my head whisper lies like, *"If my business fails, it means I'm a failure,"* or, *"I'll never escape the financial struggles of my past."* These thoughts didn't appear overnight—they were seeds planted early in my career. Left unchecked, they grew into beliefs that threatened to hold me back from my potential.

I remember a specific day when these thoughts hit me like a tidal wave. My tutoring center was going through a slow season, and I couldn't help but think, *"What if I go broke again?"* This fear wasn't just about the present—it was tied to deep-rooted anxiety from growing up with financial insecurity. The fear felt so real and overwhelming that I almost allowed it to derail my confidence. But here's what changed everything: *I caught that thought.*

This is where mindfulness became my greatest ally. Mindfulness is the practice of paying attention to your thoughts and emotions in the present moment without judgment. On that challenging day, I paused, took a deep breath, and observed my thoughts: *"What if I go broke again?"* Instead of spiraling into anxiety, I reminded myself of the truth: *"You've developed the skills, resources, and resilience to bounce back financially. You're better prepared to handle these challenges. You can create a more secure future. You are capable and prepared to handle any challenge."* By catching this thought early and reframing it, I prevented it from becoming a limiting belief.

Mindfulness doesn't remove challenges but gives you the strength and clarity to face them head-on. It helps you see that your past doesn't define your future and empowers you to rewrite the stories you tell yourself. Think of it as flipping a switch—from fear to confidence. This process, known as cognitive restructuring or thought challenging, identifies unhelpful thoughts and replaces them with more positive and realistic ones. For instance, if you think, *"I'll never be good at this,"* you can reframe it to, *"I may not be great yet, but I can improve with practice."*

the action-reflection loop

The Action-Reflection Loop is a simple yet transformative process: Act, Reflect, Adjust. Each step chips away at the lies you've believed, replacing them with empowering truths. It's not about perfection but progress—one small step at a time.

This approach is inspired by Kolb's Experiential Learning Cycle, a framework developed by educational theorist David Kolb, which emphasizes learning through experience. This structured approach can help break free from negative thought patterns and cultivate a mindset grounded in truth and growth.

Step 1: Act – Take One Small Step

The first step is to act, even when uncertainty or fear is holding you back. For me, this meant promoting my business to a broader audience, even though I felt unsure. I remember sitting at my computer, second-guessing every word of a marketing post. Doubts crept in—what if no one clicked the link or enrolled their kids in a new tutoring center? Despite my fears, I hit *"publish."* That small action not only brought in new enrollments and increased revenue but also shattered the lie that I had to be completely prepared or an expert in marketing for it to succeed. Taking that first step proved that even imperfect action can produce powerful results.

Action bypasses the endless loop of negative thinking by creating momentum. For instance, if you've been telling yourself, *"I'm not smart enough to achieve my goals,"* a minor action might be enrolling in a free course or reading an article on the topic. It's not about the size of the step; it's about moving forward.

Step 2: Reflect – Examine the Results

Once you take action, pause and reflect. What happened? How did it feel? What did you learn? Reflection connects your actions to outcomes, reinforcing that change is possible.

After taking that first step to promote my business, I noticed small but meaningful victories. A new client reached out, expressing interest and affirming the value of my services. Someone else shared my post, extending my reach in ways I hadn't expected. These moments weren't groundbreaking, but they were significant. Each one served as evidence that my fears were unfounded. Reflecting on these small wins, I saw the truth: *"People value what I have to offer, even when I don't feel completely confident."*

Step 3: Adjust – Build on What You've Learned

The final step is to adjust. Use the insights from your reflection to refine your actions and deepen your transformation. In my case, seeing small successes gave me the confidence to take bolder, more refined steps in marketing my business— something I had been avoiding because I believed *I needed to be confident in sales and marketing.*

Kolb's concept of Active Experimentation aligns perfectly with this step. Each adjustment is a chance to test new ways of thinking and acting, creating a continuous growth and learning cycle.

every action chips away at lies

The power of the Action-Reflection Loop lies in its ability to bypass fear and doubt. I didn't feel ready or confident when I started applying this method. But each small action, followed by reflection and adjustment, chipped away at the lies I believed about myself. Over time, these small steps added up, creating new patterns in my mind that reinforced truth and opened the door to new possibilities.

For example, when I sent out my first 25,000 postcards, I was terrified it would be a disaster and that no one would enroll. However, reflecting on the successful outcome gave me the courage to try again. The lie that *"I must completely understand marketing"* lost its grip each time I tried. Instead, I adopted a new belief: *"I can be successful at basic marketing."*

putting it all together

Now it's your turn to apply the **Action-Reflection Loop.** Here's how:

- Write down the lie that's holding you back.
- Take one simple, manageable step to challenge that belief.
- Do it, even if you feel uncertain or afraid.
- Pause to examine the results. What happened? What did you learn?
- Use your insights to refine your actions and build momentum.

Each time you move through the loop, you disrupt the lies holding you back and replace them with truths rooted in action and evidence.

replacing lies with truth

. . .

Replacing lies with truth is like swapping fast food for a balanced meal. It might take effort, but the results—a healthier mindset and greater resilience—are worth every bit of work.

breaking free from the lies we believe

Action helps us move forward, but lasting transformation requires a more profound shift. Now that we have learned to embrace action, we'll focus on identifying and replacing deeply rooted lies with empowering truths that guide us toward a more fulfilling and authentic life.

While action moves you forward, lasting transformation begins in the mind. To truly rewrite your narrative, you must confront the deeply rooted lies holding you back and replace them with empowering truths. By recognizing and reframing these beliefs, you can take control of your thoughts and shape your future with clarity and confidence.

the power of reframing your thoughts

Transformation begins by questioning and reframing automatic thoughts. These thoughts often feel so ingrained that we accept them without challenge, but they are not the ultimate truth. We must shine a light on them and evaluate their validity to break free from their grip.

Negative beliefs thrive on unchallenged assumptions. They whisper things like, *"You're not from this city, so they won't support you,"* or, *"People who look like you don't succeed in these spaces."* If left unchecked, these statements can become the script that quietly dictates your actions and confidence. The way to dismantle their power is through evidence.

I remember when I moved to Texas. Doubts flooded my mind: *"What if I don't belong here? What if I can't find a job? What if I can't get established?"* These thoughts ran unchecked in my mind for about a week. But one day, as I reflected on my journey, I chose to confront them.

I wrote down one harrowing thought: *"What if I'm not successful in Texas?"* Then, I began listing evidence to challenge that lie:

- I moved across states with faith, determination, and a plan—proof of my courage and vision.
- I've earned advanced degrees, each one a testament to my perseverance and expertise.
- I've thrived in challenging professional environments that would have overwhelmed the average person.
- I've risen above personal challenges and rebuilt my life stronger every time.

When I saw these accomplishments on paper, I realized the negative thought was untrue. It wasn't rooted in reality—it was a lie I had unknowingly accepted.

After reviewing the evidence, I reframed my thought: *"I am capable of success because I have proven my resilience and skill over and over again."*

challenging negative thoughts

Questioning automatic thoughts is a powerful tool. It interrupts the cycle of negativity and opens the door to empowering beliefs. The next time you catch yourself thinking a lie, pause and ask, *"Is this true?"* Examine the evidence objectively, then reframe the thought to serve you.

challenge your negative thoughts

- **Write down a negative thought** holding you back.
- **List all the reasons this thought might not be true.** Look for factual, concrete examples that contradict it.
- **Create a new, empowering belief** based on the evidence you've gathered. Write it down and say it out loud.

The Science of Reframing Your Thoughts

Challenging negative beliefs is about building confidence and is essential for mental well-being. Our thoughts, feelings, and behaviors are interconnected. When we change our thoughts, we can influence our emotions and actions. This process helps reduce anxiety, combat depression, and improve overall mental health.

Dr. Martin Seligman, the father of positive psychology, emphasizes that optimism is a skill that can be cultivated by disputing negative thoughts. Replacing pessimistic beliefs with realistic optimism enhances one's resilience and ability to navigate life's challenges. This aligns with my experience—the simple act of questioning a lie shifted my entire perspective.

challenging a deeply held belief

One of the most pivotal moments in my journey was confronting the belief that *I wasn't smart enough to succeed academically.* As a young mother returning to school, I carried the weight of self-doubt. The voice in my head constantly whispered, *"You're going to fail."* For a while, it seemed right— my first year of college ended in failure, and it took me an entire decade to complete my first degree.

But I refused to let that failure define me. Instead of giving in to fear, I decided to challenge it. I looked back on my life and found evidence that disproved the lie: times when I had learned new life skills, tackled tough situations, and adapted to challenges with determination. Each instance reminded me that I was more capable than I believed.

Gradually, I replaced *"I'm not smart enough"* with *"I am capable of learning."* This simple but powerful mindset shift unlocked doors I once thought were out of reach. With renewed determination, I went on to earn not one but two master's degrees and a PhD. Today, I approach my goals with confidence, knowing that the narrative I choose to believe shapes my success.

clearing mental toxins

Looking back, I realize this belief didn't come out of nowhere. It was rooted in emotional experiences—fear of failure from my first year of college and the pressure of being a young mother trying to prove myself. These deeply rooted experiences acted like mental toxins, quietly contaminating my thoughts and tying me to the lie that I wasn't smart enough.

Mental toxins like this often go unnoticed, but their effects are powerful. They seep into your mindset and slowly erode your confidence, holding you back from your full potential. Breaking free from them requires mindfulness and deliberate effort.

Ask yourself, *"What is feeding this belief? What past experiences might be poisoning my perspective?"* Once you've identified the source, use mindfulness to observe the thought without judgment. Recognize the toxic influence, but remind yourself that it does not define you. Then, challenge the thought with evidence and replace it with a nourishing truth.

anchoring positive beliefs in daily life

Awareness and reframing are ongoing practices. Once you've challenged a lie, it's essential to reinforce the truth. Here are some strategies:

- **Start your day with affirmations.** Speak truths that counteract negative thoughts. Example: *"I am equipped and capable."*
- **Practice gratitude.** Focus on what's working rather than dwelling on what's not.
- **Visualize success.** Picture yourself thriving, which solidifies your belief in what's possible.

Each time you refuse to accept a lie, you weaken its hold and strengthen your confidence. This process is not about pretending everything is perfect but about grounding yourself in truth rather than fear.

final thoughts

Replacing lies with truth is an ongoing journey, but it's one of the most powerful transformations you can experience. Lies create barriers, but truth sets you free. Every time you challenge a negative belief and replace it with an empowering one, you reshape your reality.

Your mind is your most powerful tool—use it wisely. Choose truth, choose growth, and choose to believe in yourself.

ancient wisdom for modern lies

. . .

Every day, countless voices compete for our attention, each claiming to hold the key to happiness, success, or validation. Social media influences how we think, often in ways we don't notice. Television reinforces ideas about identity and success. Cultural norms shape our beliefs about purpose. Many of these messages are misleading. When we accept them as truth, they distort our sense of self and weaken our confidence.

Warnings against these lies have existed for centuries. The Apostle Paul addressed similar cultural deceptions that misled entire communities. His words, written nearly 2,000 years ago, remain relevant today. He urged people to think critically and reject beliefs that are not rooted in truth. His letters challenge us to discern between deception and wisdom. By examining Paul's teachings, we can apply his insights to the lies that continue to shape modern society.

. . .

Conforming vs. Transforming

In his letter to the Romans, Paul delivered a powerful challenge: "Do not conform to the pattern of this world, but be transformed by the renewing of your mind." He understood how easily societal norms could sway people—in ancient Rome, status, power, and pleasure dictated one's worth. To fit in, individuals often compromise their values. The pressure to conform was immense, just as it is today.

Society still promotes the idea that happiness and success require meeting certain standards. Social media reinforces this belief by showcasing curated images of ideal lives, flawless appearances, and perfect relationships. The underlying message suggests that unless we conform, we are unworthy. However, Paul's words present a different perspective. Transformation does not come from blending in but from reshaping our minds. It begins with questioning what we have been taught and seeking deeper truths about who we are.

The Danger of Deceptive Philosophy

Paul's letter to the Colossians warns: "See to it that no one takes you captive through hollow and deceptive philosophy, which depends on human tradition and the elemental spiritual forces of this world rather than on Christ." The people of Colossae encountered ideas that appeared progressive and intelligent but ultimately led them away from the truth. These philosophies offered temporary satisfaction but left individuals disconnected from their deeper meaning.

Modern culture is filled with similar deceptions. We are told that wealth determines worth, that beauty guarantees happiness, and that popularity equals success. Some philosophies encourage living by "your truth," disregarding the existence of deeper, universal principles. These ideas may feel empowering, but they often lead to isolation and confusion. Paul's wisdom urges us to ask an essential question: Are the beliefs we accept based on fleeting trends or something enduring? True fulfillment comes from foundations that do not crumble with time.

Finding Stability in Truth

In his letter to the Ephesians, Paul describes the danger of being misled: "We must no longer be infants, tossed back and forth by the waves, and blown here and there by every wind of teaching and by the cunning and craftiness of people in their deceitful scheming." His words paint a clear picture of instability. When individuals lack discernment, they become vulnerable to every new trend or opinion.

The people of Ephesus lived in a thriving city filled with competing ideas. They faced the temptation to follow teachings that seemed appealing but ultimately led them away from genuine wisdom. Paul emphasized the need for maturity, which allows individuals to recognize and reject misleading beliefs.

Many people today experience this same instability. They build their identities on shifting societal standards. What is praised one day may be ridiculed the next. Social media amplifies this instability by creating environments where self-worth depends on external approval. Paul's message serves as a reminder that stability comes from rooting identity in truth rather than popular opinion. When we know who we are, we are not easily swayed.

. . .

Applying Ancient Wisdom to Modern Life

Paul's letters offer timeless guidance for navigating today's societal pressures. He challenges us to reject falsehoods and build our identities on truth. Cultural norms may suggest that validation must come from others. They may insist that past mistakes dictate the future. However, Paul's teachings encourage a different approach.

One of the most damaging lies suggests that worth is tied to external approval. Society teaches that achievement, appearance, or popularity determine value. However, Paul's message reminds us that our identity is not defined by what others think. Another common lie tells us that our past limits what we can become. Yet transformation is always possible when we renew our minds and choose a different path.

At a time when many struggle with uncertainty about their purpose, Paul's wisdom provides hope. He calls us to examine the beliefs we hold about ourselves. Lies can keep us trapped in cycles of insecurity, comparison, and self-doubt. Recognizing and rejecting these lies leads to true freedom to live confidently and authentically.

Conclusion

The warnings Paul gave centuries ago remain just as relevant today. Society will always create new versions of old lies, but the underlying deception remains the same. The pressure to conform, the lure of deceptive philosophies, and the instability of shifting beliefs continue to affect our lives.

The solution is also timeless. We can break free from harmful narratives by choosing to discern truth from falsehood, renewing our minds, and grounding ourselves in enduring principles. Paul's teachings offer more than just guidance; they empower us to reclaim our identity. Instead of being swayed by ever-changing societal messages, we can stand firm in truths that bring lasting peace and purpose.

True transformation happens when we stop believing lies and live by our truth.

resilience through self-compassion

• • •

Self-compassion is like hydration for your mind—it's essential for recovery and resilience. Without it, you risk burnout. With it, you're replenished and ready to face challenges with strength.

the strength found in self-compassion

The last chapter explored how replacing lies with truth can transform our mindset. But transformation also requires resilience. This chapter will uncover how self-compassion strengthens our ability to bounce back from challenges and keeps us moving forward with grace.

Life is a series of peaks and valleys. We all encounter setbacks, disappointments, and failures along the way. These challenges can be tough to navigate, often leaving us feeling defeated, discouraged, and even hopeless. However, resilience isn't about avoiding these obstacles—it's about navigating them with self-compassion and emerging stronger on the other side.

the lie of self-criticism vs. the power of self-compassion

When life feels overwhelming, a common lie creeps in: *"You're weak if you struggle."* This voice makes you feel guilty for feeling drained or uncertain, making problems seem impossible to resolve. Self-compassion dismantles this lie. It helps you acknowledge your struggles without judgment and treat yourself with kindness. More importantly, it allows you to rewrite your story into one of resilience and growth.

Imagine comforting a friend going through a difficult time. You wouldn't criticize them for their shortcomings or minimize their pain. Instead, you'd offer words of encouragement, remind them of their strengths, and suggest ways they could move forward. So why don't we extend the same grace to ourselves?

how self-compassion builds resilience

Resilience isn't about pushing through at all costs—it's about giving yourself the grace to recover, learn, and rise again. Here's how self-compassion strengthens resilience:

- **It dismantles unworthiness.** Struggling doesn't mean you're weak or incapable; it simply means you're human.
- **It reduces stress and anxiety.** Self-criticism fuels tension, while self-kindness fosters clarity and emotional balance.
- **It boosts motivation.** Harsh self-judgment depletes energy, but self-compassion inspires perseverance.

- **It enhances relationships.** When you treat yourself with care, extending that kindness to others becomes second nature.

rejecting lies through self-compassion

In 2016, I was nearing the end of my doctoral studies—a journey I had pursued with unwavering dedication. However, my progress was abruptly halted by a spontaneous cerebrospinal fluid leak. The condition left me bedridden, with excruciating headaches whenever I sat or stood. For months, I was confined to rest, unable to work, study, or engage in the life I had built.

As I lay in bed, the lies began to creep in: *"You're not strong enough to finish school." "You're failing, and everyone will see it."* These thoughts were relentless, amplifying my frustration and fear.

But instead of giving in, I chose to reject those lies with self-compassion. I reminded myself that my health was paramount and that my value wasn't tied to an arbitrary deadline. I acknowledged my pain, grieved my temporary loss of momentum, and allowed myself the grace to rest and heal.

This wasn't easy. It required me to confront the lie that *rest was a weakness* and replace it with the truth: *"Rest is part of resilience."* Slowly but surely, I shifted my focus from what I couldn't control to what I could: nurturing my mind, body, and spirit through self-compassion. Eventually, I returned to my studies and earned my PhD.

This experience taught me a powerful lesson: resilience doesn't mean surviving at all costs. It means rejecting the lies that tell you you're weak and choosing kindness and self-care instead.

mental toxins: recognizing and removing harmful beliefs

The lies we tell ourselves during setbacks don't come out of nowhere—they're often rooted in past experiences, fears, or societal pressures. These mental toxins act like spoiled food for the mind, feeding self-doubt and negativity.

For me, the fear of failure during my health crisis was tied to childhood experiences of needing to prove my worth. Recognizing this connection was the first step in rejecting and replacing those lies with truths.

Self-compassion helps you detoxify your thoughts by bringing awareness to these harmful patterns and challenging them. It allows you to confront the toxic lie of *"I'm not good enough"* with evidence of your strength, perseverance, and humanity.

cultivating self-compassion: practical strategies

To reject the lies of self-criticism and embrace the truth of resilience, practice these strategies:

- Notice the critical voice in your head. Ask yourself, *"Would I say this to someone I love?"* If not, reframe it.
- Engage in activities that bring comfort. Whether walking, meditating, or resting, make space for self-care.
- Replace harsh criticism with encouragement. Instead of *"I'll never figure this out,"* try *"I'm learning, and it's okay to take my time."*
- Forgive yourself. Mistakes are part of growth. Instead of dwelling on them, focus on the lessons they offer.
- Seek support. Sharing your struggles with trusted

people can remind you of your strengths and encourage you.

anchoring resilience in daily life

Self-compassion isn't a one-time fix—it's a daily practice that helps you reject lies and anchor yourself in truth. Here's how to integrate it into your routine:

- **Start your day with affirmations.** *"I am strong, capable, and resilient."*
- **Practice gratitude.** Shift your focus from what's wrong to what's right.
- **Visualize success.** Picture yourself overcoming challenges with confidence.

As a young mother, I worked tirelessly to provide for my children, often holding down multiple jobs while returning to school. I poured everything into giving them a better life. But there were moments when I fell short. I wasn't always there in the ways I wanted to be, and there were days when I questioned whether I was doing enough.

Years later, as my children became adults, they shared their perspectives on my parenting—some of which were hard to hear. They pointed out my absences. When I was working instead of being present with them, those conversations were painful, but they also taught me something important: self-compassion was the only way to navigate my past without shame.

I told them the truth: *"I did the best I could with what I had at the time."* And I meant it. Self-compassion helped me accept my imperfections and allowed me to be open, honest, and loving with my children, even in difficult conversations.

resilience in the face of adversity

Life will always have challenges, but resilience is built when you choose compassion over criticism. It's built when you acknowledge your efforts and progress, even when the results aren't perfect. It's built when you forgive yourself for your mistakes and use them as stepping stones to grow stronger.

closing thoughts

As you face your challenges, remember this: You are doing the best you can with what you have. Resilience doesn't require perfection; it requires persistence and self-compassion. Reject the lies that tell you you're not enough or that your struggles make you weak.

Embrace the truth that every setback is an opportunity to rise, stronger and more self-aware than before. Show yourself the kindness and understanding you deserve. Let self-compassion be the foundation of your resilience, and watch how it transforms your life and relationships.

True strength lies not in the absence of struggle but in your ability to rise above it with courage, self-compassion, and unwavering belief in your capacity to heal and grow.

the power of
visualization

. . .

Visualization is like planning your meals—it sets you up for success. When you picture your goals clearly, you're choosing to feed your mind with intention, ensuring it gets the nourishment it needs to thrive.

---

seeing your future before it happens

Building resilience through self-compassion opens the door to a brighter future. This chapter will explore visualization, a powerful tool for aligning thoughts, actions, and energy with dreams. Learn how to see the future you desire and take steps to make it a reality.

Visualization is one of the most powerful tools for transforming dreams into reality. It involves creating mental images of where you want to go, who you want to be, and what you want to achieve. When you consistently picture your goals, you align your thoughts and actions with your aspirations. This makes your goals feel more tangible and achievable.

the power of seeing it before you achieve it

The saying goes, *"You have to see it before you see it."* Visualization is about creating that vision in your mind before it manifests in reality. For me, visualization has been one of the keys to my success. Many of the milestones I've achieved began as images in my mind.

I remember when I first envisioned opening my tutoring center. I pictured myself unlocking the doors long before I had the keys. I could see the students walking in, their faces lighting up as they learned. I imagined the desks, the colors of the walls, and the energy of a space dedicated to growth. That vision became my anchor. On difficult days when doubt crept in, I leaned into that mental picture, reminding myself that my dream was already taking shape—I just needed to keep going.

The same was true when I saw myself as a school principal. Before I stepped into the role, I pictured myself walking the halls, making impactful decisions, and creating a space where students and teachers thrived. I didn't just dream about the title; I visualized the work, the interactions, and the changes I wanted to make. That vision pulled me forward and shaped my actions until the day it became a reality.

And today, I do the same with my writing and speaking career. I visualize standing on stage, sharing my books, and inspiring audiences. I see the people in the crowd and their expressions of understanding and empowerment. I hear the applause, feel the connection, and remind myself that what I am working toward is already done in my mind—it's just a matter of bringing it to life.

how visualization works

Visualization isn't magic, but it feels magical in how it channels focus and intention. When you visualize, your brain creates neural pathways that make the imagined scenario feel real. This process increases confidence and motivation, helping you take the necessary steps to achieve your goals. Visualization also primes your mind to notice opportunities that align with your aspirations, acting as a magnet for the resources and connections you need.

practical steps to harness visualization

If you want to use visualization to achieve your goals, here's how to get started:

1. Define Your Vision
Be clear about what you want. Whether it's a career milestone, a personal achievement, or a lifestyle change, take time to articulate your goals in detail.

2. Create a Mental Image
Close your eyes and picture yourself achieving your goal. What does it look like? How do you feel? Engage all your senses to make the image as vivid as possible.

3. Make It a Daily Practice
Dedicate a few minutes each day to visualize your goals. Morning and evening are great times to do this, as your mind is more receptive.

4. Pair Visualization with Action
While visualization sets the stage, action brings the vision to life.

Identify and commit to steps that will move you closer to your goal.

5. Reflect and Adjust

As you visualize and act, take time to reflect on your progress. Are there new opportunities or challenges? Adjust your mental images and actions to stay aligned with your goals.

my personal visualization practice

Visualization isn't just something I do occasionally; it's an integral part of my life. When I visualize, I create a mental movie of my future. I see myself walking through the halls of success, confidently speaking, and making a positive impact. I don't just see the result; I imagine the journey—the work, the growth, the learning.

For example, when I pictured myself as a school principal, I didn't just imagine wearing the title. I saw myself interacting with teachers, encouraging students, and making decisions that shaped the school's future. By envisioning the full scope of the role, I prepared myself mentally and emotionally for the challenges and responsibilities that came with it.

turning dreams into reality

One of the most rewarding aspects of visualization is watching your dreams unfold in real life. It reminds you of the power of intention and the importance of aligning your thoughts, words, and actions. Whether I was becoming a principal, owning tutoring centers, or speaking in front of audiences, each vision I held in my mind's eye became a stepping stone toward my current reality.

As I visualize discussing my books with audiences, I see the next chapter of my journey taking shape. I picture readers finding hope, inspiration, and practical strategies in my words. I see myself standing on stages, connecting with people from all walks of life, and empowering them to transform their thinking and achieve their goals. This vision fuels my current work and reminds me why I began this journey.

the truth about visualization

Visualization alone won't guarantee success, but it sets the stage for it. It creates clarity, boosts confidence, and primes your mind for action. The real power lies in combining visualization with consistent effort and a willingness to embrace challenges.

If you've never tried visualization, start small. Picture yourself achieving a goal you've been working toward. See it, feel the emotions associated with success, and use that energy to take your next step. Remember, every great accomplishment begins as a vision. The more vividly you can see it, the closer you are to making it a reality.

final thoughts

Your mind is your greatest tool! When you intentionally shape your vision, you give your brain a blueprint to follow. Visualization is not about wishful thinking—it's about creating a strong mental reality that your actions naturally align with.

Take a moment today. Close your eyes. See yourself achieving the goal that's been sitting in your heart. Feel the success, the joy, the accomplishment. Then ask yourself: *What small step can I take today to bring this vision to life?* Because the future you desire is already waiting—it just needs you to believe in it enough to take action.

creating new habits

. . .

Habits are like the staples of your mental diet. They're the healthy choices you make daily that build a foundation for long-term growth. Consistency in your habits ensures you're constantly feeding your mind with what it needs to flourish.

---

the small habits that shape a big life

Visualization provides the clarity needed to pursue your goals, but lasting success depends on daily habits. Small, intentional actions shape your life and reinforce the truths you've embraced. By building these habits, you create a strong foundation for sustained growth.

Habits shape our lives. They define our routines, influence our thoughts, and determine our outcomes. The good news is that small, intentional habits can lead to life-changing transformations when practiced consistently. It's not about massive overhauls but making small, meaningful changes that build momentum over time.

the unexpected power of making my bed

Making my bed every morning was one of the most life-changing habits I developed. Who knew this mundane task could double as a life coach? At first glance, it might not seem like much. But this small, intentional act became a cornerstone of my day. It wasn't just about tidying up my space but creating a routine that set the tone for my mornings.

Making my bed taught me discipline and consistency. Who knew a few seconds of fluffing pillows and smoothing sheets could unlock such wisdom? Each day, I started with a small accomplishment that created a ripple effect. It became a mental signal to treat myself well, to prioritize my needs, and to invest my best energy into myself. It also gave me a sense of control and order, especially when life felt chaotic. Over time, this simple habit became a foundation for building discipline and consistency in other areas of my life. It turns out my bed wasn't just a place for rest—it was my first teacher in the school of 'Get Your Life Together.'

the power of starting small

Creating new habits doesn't require grand gestures. The most sustainable habits often start small. Waking up early, making your bed, or spending 30 minutes in quiet reflection each morning may seem insignificant. However, these small actions build discipline and create a sense of accomplishment that grows over time.

When you commit to a small habit and stick to it, you prove to yourself that you can change. This builds confidence and creates momentum, making it easier to tackle bigger goals. The key is consistency—showing up for yourself every day, even when it feels inconvenient or unnecessary.

tools for success

Developing new habits requires intention and strategy. Here are some tools to help you succeed:

1. Track Your Progress
Use a physical or digital habit tracker to monitor your progress. Visualizing your consistency can be incredibly motivating.

2. Set Reminders
Set up reminders on your phone, calendar, or planner to prompt you to engage in your habit. These nudges can help you stay on track, especially in the beginning.

3. Reflect on Your Habits
Take a few minutes each day or week to reflect on how your habits impact your life. What's working? What could be adjusted? Reflection helps you stay mindful and motivated.

4. Pair Habits Together
Pair your new habit with an existing one. For example, if you're already brushing your teeth every morning, use that moment as a cue to say an affirmation or visualize your goals.

spending time with yourself first

One of the greatest lessons I learned from making my bed was the importance of spending time with myself first. This simple habit reminded me to prioritize my well-being before pouring energy into others. Whether it's through meditation, journaling, or simply enjoying a quiet moment, starting the day with yourself sets a powerful tone. It reinforces the message that you are worthy of your time and attention.

Treating yourself well equips you to show up for others. You'll be more focused, grounded, and confident. Investing in yourself isn't selfish; it's necessary for showing up fully in all areas of your life.

Align Your Thoughts with Truth

A practical way to incorporate new habits into your life is to set a daily reminder to check in with your thoughts. Ask yourself, *"Are my thoughts aligned with the truth? Am I focusing on possibilities rather than limitations?"* Use this moment to course-correct and reinforce positive thinking.

For example, if you notice a negative thought creeping in, challenge it with an affirmation or reframe it with evidence-based reasoning. This small, daily check-in can help you stay grounded and focused on your goals.

building momentum

The beauty of habits is that they compound over time. What starts as a small, daily action can evolve into a transformative practice that impacts every area of your life. For example:

- **Making your bed** might lead to a greater focus on cleanliness and organization.
- **Practicing gratitude daily** might lead to a more optimistic outlook.
- **Committing to 10 minutes of reading** might become a lifelong love for learning.

Each habit you develop builds on the last, creating a powerful chain of positive change.

a life built on habits

The habits you cultivate today shape the person you become tomorrow. Start small, stay consistent, and trust the process. Whether it's making your bed, practicing gratitude, or checking in with your thoughts, each habit is a step toward becoming the best version of yourself.

final thoughts

The key to creating new habits is not perfection but persistence. Each new habit you build is a rejection of the lie that you can't change or grow. Show up for yourself every day, and over time, you'll see the remarkable impact of these small, intentional actions. Who knew life's greatest lessons could come from something as simple as straightening your sheets?

own the truth, reject the lies

. . .

You made it. You've walked through every chapter, confronted the lies, and uncovered the truth about who you are, what you're capable of, and where you're headed. But now comes the real test—the part that separates those who merely consume information from those who apply it and transform their lives.

Because here's the truth: knowing the lies is not enough. Recognizing the truth is not enough. Transformation only happens when you act on it.

Think about everything we've exposed in this book. Lies about your worth. Lies about success. Lies about failure, approval, time, and identity. You now see how these deceptive thoughts sneak into your mind, shaping your decisions, limiting your potential, and keeping you stuck. But you have the power to stop the cycle. You can reject what doesn't serve you and build a new mindset that aligns with your purpose.

your mind is your most valuable asset

Your thoughts are not just thoughts—they are the architects of your future. They dictate your emotions, decisions, and, ultimately, your destiny. If you allow lies to dictate your thinking, you will live a life smaller than what was meant for you. But when you align your mind with truth, you step into a power that can reshape everything—your finances, confidence, relationships, and success.

There's a reason so many people never reach their full potential. It's not because they aren't talented or smart enough. It's because they never challenge the thoughts that keep them small. They continue to believe they are stuck, too late, unworthy, or incapable.

But that's not your story anymore.

Your story is one of breakthroughs. Your story is one of renewal. Your story is one of power.

decide who you will be from this day forward

Now, I want to challenge you: Who will you be after this book? Will you return to the old patterns, allowing lies to run your life? Or will you develop this new awareness and build your future on truth?

Success comes from shifting your identity and mindset. People who succeed don't eat the lie that they're not good enough. People who build wealth don't eat the lie that money is evil or unreachable. People who live with purpose don't eat the lie that they need the approval of others.

If you want abundance, confidence, and impact, you must think, speak, and act differently. Truth alone won't change your life; applied truth will.

this is your moment

This book wasn't written for people who want to stay the same. It was written for people who are **ready to break free.** If that's you, then here's what you must do next:

1. **Reject the Lies.** Every time a limiting belief creeps in, shut it down. Say out loud: *That's a lie, and I refuse to believe it.*
2. **Affirm the Truth.** Speak life over yourself daily. Say: *I am capable. I am worthy. I am designed for success.*
3. **Take Action.** Stop waiting for the "right time." Start today—whether that's writing the book, launching the business, setting the boundary, or making the investment.
4. **Surround Yourself With Truth.** Get in rooms with people who **challenge your thinking and demand your growth.** Stop hanging around those who reinforce the lies.
5. **Stay Committed.** This is not a one-time decision. It's a daily practice. **Choose truth every day until it becomes the foundation of your identity.**

The world doesn't need another person trapped in fear, waiting for permission to step into their calling. The world needs you—fully confident, fully free, and fully committed to becoming everything you were created to be.

So what's it going to be? Will you keep eating the lies, or will you start feeding your mind the truth?

Because transformation is a choice, and that choice is yours.

Don't eat that lie. Choose the truth. Choose your future.

And never look back.

your thoughts/reflections

afterword

The **Action-Reflection Loop** is a powerful tool for breaking free from fear and doubt. You create a continuous growth cycle by choosing **action over thought**, reflecting on your experiences, and adjusting based on your learning. Each step chips away at the lies you've believed, building a mindset grounded in truth and possibility.

Remember, you don't need to feel ready to take the first step. Start small, stay consistent, and trust the process. Every action you take sends a clear message to your mind: *"I am capable. I am growing. I am enough."*

about the author

Dr. Alice Ward-Johnson is a powerhouse in mindset transformation, personal development, and success coaching. As the author of **More Than Enough: A Guide to Achieving Your Goals**, she has inspired countless individuals to break free from limiting beliefs and step into their full potential.

With a PhD in Education and over 20 years of experience as an educator, entrepreneur, and speaker, Dr. Johnson has dedicated her life to helping people shift their mindset to achieve their goals. Her expertise spans **goal achievement, mindset shifts, and personal growth**, blending practical strategies with deep wisdom to create lasting change.

In **Don't Eat That Lie: Exposing the Myths That Hold You Back and Rewiring Your Mind for Success**, Dr. Johnson delivers an unapologetic wake-up call to those ready to stop settling and start thriving. Her engaging style, personal stories, and actionable insights empower readers to rewire their thinking and create a life built on truth, confidence, and purpose.

Beyond her work as an author and speaker, Dr. Johnson is the founder of **Fulcrum Mindset**, where she helps individuals and organizations unlock their potential through coaching, courses, and leadership training.

Whether through her books, speaking engagements, or

coaching, her message remains the same: **You can do this! You are more than enough!**

www.ingramcontent.com/pod-product-compliance
Lightning Source LLC
Chambersburg PA
CBHW071528120626
46550CB00006B/2389